SOCIALISM UNMASKED

Who propagated it--how and why

I0141027

By A. N. FIELD,

Author of "The Truth About The Slump" "All These Things" &c.

Published by A. N. FIELD,

Box 154   NELSON   New Zealand

ISBN: 978-2-925369-47-9
Printed in the USA.

This pamphlet is a reprint of the Supplement to the No. 4 issue of the Examiner, February, 1938.

Facts About The Bank of England

6d. posted.

An amazing story revealed by search of official records, showing the constitution and policies of this financial secret society controlling the British Empire.

All These Things

By A. N. Field.

This book shows how underground influences made the World War of 1914-18; how Governments are controlled by hidden forces; how booms and slumps are made; and how industry is being insidiously enslaved. The names and particulars of the men concerned are given, and the authority for every statement of consequence.

"A terrific indictment: one of the most convincing books I have ever read."—A U.S.A. constitutional lawyer.

"The most valuable contribution to modern history we have as regards the British people."—An English author who has written on these matters for years.

Price 6s. (also in cloth at 8s 6d), post free if ordered direct.

A. N. Field, Box 154, Nelson, New Zealand.

Obtainable also from The Britons Publishing Society, 40 Great Ormond St., London, W.C. 2, and from Messrs. Madison and Marshall, Inc., 48 East 48th St., New York.

Most people look upon Socialism as a great democratic movement that has grown up spontaneously. The actual facts are here presented. There is nothing in the least democratic about Socialism, although it makes much play with the word "Democracy". Its history is a story of subterfuge and intrigue; of tiny minorities engineering themselves into control of apathetic majorities.

As will be seen, it is extremely doubtful whether Karl Marx, prophet of modern Socialism, had any sincere belief in the theories he propounded. He preached a gospel of plunder and violence, and later sought to manufacture a "scientific" basis for it, which basis will not hold water.

Just as business-men have been deluded into supporting the present money system, so trades unionists have been propagandised into supporting Socialism. Both things operate to exactly the same end, the concentration of all control in the hands of small minority, and the reduction of the rest of the population to propertyless serfdom.

I

Karl Marx, Apostle of Hatred

Modern Socialism dates from February 23, 1848, when the Communist Manifesto of Marx and Engels was flung forth on the very day the revolution against the Orleans Monarchy began in France.

Marx in this manifesto called upon the workers to rise in violent revolution. "The Communists," he declared, "disdain to conceal their views and aims. They openly declare that their ends can be attained only by the forcible overthrow of existing social conditions. Let the ruling classes tremble at a Communistic revolution. The proletarians have nothing to lose but their chains. They have a world to win. Workers of all lands, unite!"

Up to this time Socialism had been based on brotherly love for the poor and oppressed, and its practical effort was directed to the founding of Socialist utopias, all of which failed dismally. Marx fused Socialism with the underground Communist movement, preaching a general massacre of the "possessing classes."

Finance Aids Revolution

The year 1848 in which Marx launched his gospel of plunder and hatred was one of great distress and revolution throughout Europe. That distress was largely consequent on a money juggle in Britain in 1844, when the Bank Charter Act tied the currency up rigidly with gold. This was followed in 1847 by the greatest monetary crisis Britain had known up to that time, the effects of which were felt throughout all Europe. After tracing out the course of events in detail, Sir Archibald Alison said in his "History of Europe" (2nd series, vol. vii; 1858):

"The suspension of credit, want of employment, and stagnation of industry among the workmen of Paris, which proved fatal to the Orleans dynasty, had its origin in the Bank Charter Act of London. .. It has led to the overthrow of the monarchies of Austria and Prussia."

The crisis produced revolutionary outbreaks also in Italy, and the abortive Chartist rising in Britain. Finance and revolution, then as now, went hand in hand: one preparing the ground for the other.

Karl Marx was thirty years old when he produced the Communist Manifesto. What sort of a man was he? "First and foremost," says Professor F. J. C. Hearnshaw in his "Survey of Socialism" (Macmillan, 1929), "he was a Jew by race, the descendant of a long line of rabbis whose proper name was not Marx but Mordechai. In 1824, when he was six years of age, his father, for political reasons, abandoned Judaism for a nominal Christianity."

A Life of Intrigue and Rows

Marx's father was a lawyer, and his brother-in-law was the reactionary Prussian Minister of State von Westphalen. He received a university education and never did a day's manual labour in his life—the only sort of labour that is worth anything according to the Marxian gospel. After editing a newspaper which the Prussian Government suppressed, Marx went to Paris in 1843 and took up revolutionary plotting with Bakunin, the Russian Anarchist, and Engels. By 1849 he was settled in Britain where he remained most of the time until his death in 1883. For many years he lived on a dole of £350 a year given him by his friend Engels, who had become proprietor of a Lancashire cotton

4

mill. There is suspicion that the £350 really came from the Prussian Government to keep Marx going in his efforts to stir up trouble in Britain.

Of Marx's character, Mazzini. the Italian revolutionary long acquainted with him, said: "Hatred outweighs love in his heart." Bakunin, with whom he had long worked, said of him: "He was a vain man, perfidious and artful." Schurz in his "Reminiscenses" said: "I have never seen a man whose bearing was so provoking and intolerable. . . He had a most obnoxious faculty for seeing the worst in all persons whom he met; and all with whom he quarrelled were denounced in language of unmitigated virulence as traitors or as fools." Spargo in his life of Marx gave details of fourteen prolonged and embittered brawls of Marx with his fellow revolutionaries. Mrs. Webster in "The Surrender of an Empire" says an old Socialist well acquainted with the family told her no more miserable women could be imagined than Marx's daughters, two of whom ended by committing suicide.

"Scientific" Socialism

The whole essence of Marxism is in the Communist Manifesto, and centres round the class war. Later on "Das Kapital" was written by Marx to provide a scientific basis for his incitement to plunder and violence. This "scientific" side rests on the theory that everything in history is due to economic causes. Religion, patriotism, devotion to ideal causes, martyrdoms, spiritualities, simply do not count at all, and influence no man's actions. If they are admitted as factors in history Marxism crumbles down in a heap of dust. Even the Jewish Socialist, Professor Laski, is constrained to confess that this economic or materialist interpretation of history is "radically false". It is undoubted rubbish. Humanity does not begin and end with the belly.

5

In the first volume of "Das Kapital" Marx justified his programme of loot by his "Theory of Surplus Value", which, although wrapped up in mazes of words, simply boils down to an assertion that labour produces all and therefore the labourer is entitled to all, and that the value of an article is the labour time expended on it, regardless of whether or not anybody wants the article when it is made. According to this, a rat-trap that won't catch rats is worth as much as one that will, if the same labour time was spent in making it.

Even the faithful could not reconcile this preposterous theory with the facts, and they were promised a vindication of it in the later volumes of "Das Kapital". When the final volume came out in 1894 after Marx's death it was found that Marx himself had virtually thrown overboard the theory that is the corner-stone of Socialism, and which still goes on getting votes for Socialists all the time on the cry of "Everything for the workers". As to what is a fair and just division of the proceeds of industry—the kernel of the whole problem—Socialism has not one solitary word to say. As an economic theory it is a hopeless affair. As an incitement to plunder it is most highly efficient.

Other People's Thunder

Marx built up his books by laborious research in the British Museum, and later investigators have discovered that he plundered wholesale from other writers without the least acknowledgment, dishonestly passing off huge chunks out of their writings as his own. Dr. A. Menger and Professor Foxwell in "The Right to the Whole Produce of Labour" (1899) showed in detail Marx's wholesale stealing from the treatises and pamphlets of Ricardo, McCulloch, Hall, Owen, Thompson, Hodgskin, Gray all without acknowledgment and often with unscrupulous distortion to make them fit his argument.

6

Professor Hearnshaw, whose book is well worth reading, says it is hard to avoid the conclusion that Marx knew the fallacy and even the absurdity of the theories he propounded in his books, and that he deliberately wrapped them up in ambiguous words to prevent others seeing through them. Dr. Bohm-Bauwerck, a well-known European economist, similarly expressed the opinion that Marx's books obviously consisted of matter put together as artificial support for views previously arrived at on different grounds altogether.

A Faked Concoction

A former Jewish Bolshevik Commissar, Morris Gordin, told how he came to see that the whole Marxist theory is a fake. Mr. Gordin, after acting as editor of the Communist organ in America, went to Russia in 1921 and was chief of the Communist Press Bureau in Moscow until 1924. Becoming dissatisfied with Communism in practice in Russia, he retired into Moscow University to study Marx. He told the Union League of Michigan in an address delivered in Detroit on January 16, 1931, that he there discovered that Marx and Engels had concocted their theories first and then in after years hunted around for facts to fit them. "My Communism," he said, "dropped down dead on the spot."*

II

The Gospel of Destruction

The Communist Manifesto remains to-day the whole thing in Marxian Socialism, and it is nothing at all but the preaching of plunder and violence. As Professor Hearnshaw says in his book:

"It held out a prospect of revenge, destruction, and sanguinary devastation—the overthrow and

*For exact sources of citations not in text in this section refer to Professor Hearnshaw's "Survey of Socialism".

humiliation of thrones, aristocracies, and above all
the hated bourgeoisie—that appealed with irresist-
ible attraction to the passions of envy, hatred and
malice which filled Marx and his associates with
fanatical and truly diabolical fury. The energy and
vigour of the Communist Manifesto is the demoniac
energy of the madman, possessed by the evil spirits
of jealousy, greed, lust of power, and the insane
hunger of revenge in respect of imaginary wrongs."

Among his numerous hatreds Marx included
both patriotism and Christianity. "Religion is the
opium of the people," he said in much-quoted words.
Socialism is a materialist view of the universe which
is quite incompatible with a belief in Christianity;
and although some sentimental people affect to reconcile the two, the leading Communists and Socialists have never had any doubts on the matter. As
Herr Bebel, German Socialist leader, put it years
ago, "Christianity and Socialism stand toward each
other as fire and water."

Blood and More Blood!

If Marx hated Christianity, his fellow-Jew and
fellow-Socialist, Ferdinand Lassalle, founder of
German political Socialism, left on record his hatred
of Christians as well. The London "Morning Post"
book, "The Cause of World Unrest" (Grant Rich-
ards, 1920) quoted extracts from Lassalle's diary
published by Herr Paul Lindau. One recorded Lassalle as saying:

"The time will soon be at hand when, in very
deed, we will help ourselves with Christian blood."

Many people have been deluded into believing
that the colossal massacres of the Marxian Bolshevik revolution in Russia were an accidental ex-
cresence, and not an integral part of the revolutionary programme, Lenin and company really being

8

nice kindly people who would not willingly hurt a fly. Nothing is further from the truth.

The Bolshevik programme was, and is, essentially one of murder. There is ample evidence of this from many quarters. For instance, in his book "Traitors Within" (1933) former Detective Inspector Herbert T. Finch of Scotland Yard, recorded that thirty years previously he had concealed himself in a room and heard Lenin and Trotsky addressing what was supposed to be a meeting of "foreign barbers of London". He heard Lenin declaim:

"It must be bloodshed on a colossal scale . . . We must revolt, and when we revolt there shall be no mercy. . . In Russia first, and then from one side of Europe to the other. . . They must perish, down to the man who keeps a stall in the street."

Death-Dealing Trotsky

The Jew Trotsky (real name Bronstein) has written a book in advocacy of terrorism, and when the programme of wholesale massacre was launched in Russia, his speech ordering it was thus reported in the "Red Gazette" official organ of the Red Army, Petrograd, of September 1, 1918:

"We will harden our hearts into iron, we will temper them in the fire of endurance and in the blood of the enemies of Liberty. We will be cruel, hard, pitiless, until we feel no pity and are unmoved by the sight of our enemies' blood. We will open wide all the outlets for sentiment. Without pity, sparing nothing, we will massacre our enemies by hundreds. We will drown them by thousands in their own blood. For the blood of Lenin [just wounded by the Jewess Dora Kaplan], Uritzky, Zinovieff, and Volodarski, let us shed torrents of the bourgeois blood, more blood, MORE BLOOD!"*

The London "Times" of September 1, 1922, pub-

*Vide London "Fascist" August 1932.

9

lished a despatch from Riga saying: "According to Bolshevist figures the Tcheka executed 1,766,118 persons before being renamed the supreme political administration last February." The late Lord Sydenham in the House of Lords in 1923 computed the total loss of life consequent on the Russian revolution, by killings, famine and disease, as then in excess 20 million souls. Many more millions have since been slaughtered and starved to death. Since the Marxist revolutionary Socialistic doctrine has been applied in Spain on exactly the same lines of death-dealing.

To Conquer the World

When people take up with Socialism they are really linking up directly or indirectly with a movement that is essentially of Jewish origin in its conception and execution. This movement wiped out capitalists in Russia and put revolutionaries in possession, and a list of 545 of these early Bolshevik officials showed 454 of them to be Jews.† Behind these Jews were Jewish international financiers putting up the money for the undertaking. The control has been predominantly Jewish throughout.

Marx as a young man belonged to the Jewish Union for Civilisation and Science, a society holding that the Jewish nation was destined to conquer the world. One of his associates in this, Baruch Levy, wrote to him:

"In this new organisation of humanity, the sons of Israel . . will everywhere without opposition become the directing element, particularly if they can succeed in imposing on the masses of the workers the leadership of some of their number. The governments of the nations . . . will thus all pass, without out any effort, into Jewish hands, thanks to the

†Vide list compiled by Victor E. Marsden, "Morning Post" correspondent in Russia: reprinted in full in "The Defender" (Wichita Kansas) August 1934.

victory of the proletariat. Private property will be suppressed by the governors of Jewish race who will everywhere administer the public wealth. Thus will be realised the promise of the Talmud that when the times of the Messiah come the Jews will hold under their keys the property of all the people of the world."‡

Having taken this glimpse at the origins of modern Socialism, we will next see how the British Trade Unions were induced to take up with this highly non-British movement.

III.

Out of the Soho Dustbin

British Socialism—so far as there is anything British about Socialism—was born in Soho, London. And if you pick up any guide book you will learn that Soho, between Leicester Square and Oxford street, was for many years "almost entirely occupied by foreigners." A considerable percentage of these foreigners have always been agitators deported from their countries of origin for their countries' good.

In the autumn of 1880 "a few English members of the foreign Rose Street Club in Soho" set to work to propagate Socialism in England. The leader of the group was Mr. H. M. Hyndman, a wealthy man and a Cambridge University graduate, who had previously been working with Mazzini, the Italian revolutionary. Associated with him were a number of well-to-do people like himself, and a few old Chartists.

This was the beginning of what in 1884 became the Social Democratic Federation. In 1882 a band of "Christian Socialists" joined up. George Lans-

---

‡Vide Rev. Dr. Denis Fahey's "Mystical Body of Christ in the Modern World" (Browne and Nolan, Dublin, 1935)

11

bury being among the number. Later came John Burns, Tom Mann, Annie Besant and Ben Tillett. Hyndman records that the movement soon developed, as he had hoped, into "a thorough-going revolutionary organisation."

Marx Clique Busy

The Marx family presently cut in, in the person of Eleanor Marx, daughter of Karl Marx, and her "husband" Professor Aveling. They brought along in tow an Austrian Anarchist, Andreas Scheu, in order to pep up the organisation. Then they split off with William Morris, the poet, and others, and started an opposition Socialist League, because Hyndman would not obey the orders of Engels, Karl Marx's partner. This began a feud that lasted until 1892, by which time the seceders appeared to have become scared of the Anarchists who had filled up their league, and came back again.

Hot on the heels of the Hyndman organisation came the Fabian Society. This was a West End, upper crust affair from the first, and began, not in Soho, but in the more elevated atmosphere of Chelsea. Soho, however, presently took charge (as will be seen in the next section), and has held control down to the present day, except for one brief rebellion.

The Fabian Society began with the visit to London of Thomas Davidson, a Scottish "philosopher" and violent freethinker, who had been running an ethical class for Russian Jews in New York, and had visions of founding a "Fellowship of the New Life" in London. On January 4, 1884, at the lodgings of Mr. E. R. Pease, a member of the London Stock Exchange, the group which had been sitting at the feet of Davidson formed themselves into the Fabian Society, the name being suggested by the spiritualist, Frank Podmore.

Cranks to the Fore

Membership of this society consisted from the first mainly of civil servants, journalists, and professional people. Its first tract, it is true, is said to have been written by W. L. Phillips, a house painter, but Mr. Pease in his Fabian history says Mr. Phillips was the sole representative of the working classes in the organisation. Prominent among early members was the wife of a successful architect; a Mr. and Mrs. Glide Stapleton, who drove to the meetings in their own brougham; and Mrs. Charlotte Wilson, wife of a stockbroker living at Hampstead, who later dropped Socialism to take up Anarchism along with Prince Kropotkin and ran the Anarchists' newspaper for them. The dominant forces in the organisation entered in the persons of Mr. Bernard Shaw, then a young journalist, and Mr. Sidney Webb, then a clerk in the Colonial Office.

The Fabian Society from the start adopted a system of propagating Socialism by wire-pulling from behind the scenes. It began this work by modestly getting up debates in Workmen's Clubs, etc., and thus embarked on its extensive and successful programme of insinuating Socialism into every sort of organisation—and, usually, without calling it Socialism. The actual membership of the society has never been large, but it has been, and still is, a most influential and sinister body. The London "Evening Standard" of November 1, 1930, said many Labour members were then talking of the way the Fabian Society dominated the Ramsay Mac-Donald Labour Government of that time. Many people thought the Society was dead, but actually it was small, but influential, with 5000 members, said the "Evening Standard", adding:

A White-Anted Ministry

"Yet practically every recent appointment, either to high or low office, in the Labour Administration has been made from the membership of the Society. the latest examples of which are the new Air Minister, Lord Amulree, and the new Solicitor-General, Sir Stafford Cripps. I am told that at least 90 per cent of the members of the Government are in the rolls of the Society, and that, contrary to regulations, so are a good many highly-placed Civil Servants. . . This ascendancy is, of course, due to the all-powerful influence of Lord Passfield and his wife, Mrs. Sidney Webb, with whom the Fabian Society has been the passion of their lives."

The Fabian Society worked for years with drawingroom meetings in the West End. At the same time it began "permeating" the British Liberal Party and having its candidates stand as Liberals (all Fabians being pledged to Socialism) ; and it set to work on the local bodies, pushing in candidates and never minding what they were called so long as they went in to get through Socialistic measures.

Permeation of Oxford and Cambridge Universities was begun at an early date, and by 1912 this was so far advanced that Mr. Clifford Allen (now Lord Allen of Hurtwood) of the Cambridge Fabian Society, was able to launch the University Socialist Federation. In the Great War, Clifford Allen, as related in the Examiner of September, 1937, became the leader of the conscientious objectors, with funds estimated at half a million at his disposal for assisting those who wished to dodge military service on "conscientious" grounds. The seepage of Pink and Red ideas through the university colleges of New Zealand and the British Empire generally is testimony to the efficacy of the Fabian Society "permeation". The virus runs right through from the British Universities to primary school teachers in country towns in New Zealand.

The Marxist Factory

An outstanding effort of the Fabian Society on

14

the educational side was the founding of the London School of Economics in 1894 on the initiative, as usual, of Mr. Sidney Webb. This later received a handsome endowment under the will of Sir Ernest Cassel, the Jewish international financier, founder of the Vickers armament combine, and former partner with the late Jacob Schiff, of Kuhn, Loeb and Co, New York, who was mixed up both in the founding of the United States Federal Reserve system and the financing of the Russian revolution.

The late Lord Haldane, long a friend of Mr. Webb's, says he induced Sir Edward Cassel to give the money for this institution. Professor J. H. Morgan. K.C., in the "Quarterly Review" for January, 1929. says he once asked Lord Haldane why the endowment had been given, and Lord Haldane replied: "Our object is to make this institution a place to raise and train the bureaucracy of the future Socialist State."

This London School of Economics is now attached to the University of London and is in receipt of a Government grant. In his book "The Alien Menace" (4th ed., 1933), Lieut. Col. A. H. Lane pointed out that about a third of its teachers at the time he wrote bore names of highly foreign flavour—De Paula, Eckhard, Laski, Lauterpracht, Malinowski, Ginsberg, etc., etc. The school is notorious as a hive of Pink and Red propagandism.

IV.
"The Firm of Webb"

Mr. Sidney Webb, now Lord Passfield, has been throughout the guiding spirit of the Fabian Society and chief Socialist wire-puller of the British Empire. A pamphlet. "The Firm of Webb" (Boswell Press, London), gives from different sources interesting particulars about him. His appearance was

15

thus described in the diary of his wife (then Miss Beatrice Potter) under date of February 14, 1890, as published in that lady's book, 'My Apprenticeship":

"Sidney Webb, the Socialist, dined here (Devonshire House Hotel) . . . A remarkable little man, .with a huge head and a tiny body . . . A Jewish nose, prominent eyes and mouth, black hair, somewhat unkempt, spectacles and a most bourgeois black coat, shiny with wear. . . He is utterly disinterested."

"The Firm of Webb" states that Lord Passfield's birth certificate reveals that he was born at 44 Cranbourn Street, Soho, London, in 1859, and that his father was one Charles Webb, a hairdresser. In 1859 there resided in Cranbourn Street— a street with less than fifty houses in it—persons named Balague, Klyberg, Lescochi, Paillard, ·Perocchy, Kuper, Deroy, Genese, Distin, Samorini, Kammerer, Felix, Delgarre and Gouriet (vide 1859 London Directory).

Adolphe Smith, interpreter at the First and Second Internationals, is quoted as writing: "The Communists, on arriving in London, sought for lodgings . . . in the dingy streets between Soho Square and Lecester Square." If Mr Webb's boyhood were passed in this locality his environment was not exactly 100 per cent. British. "Who's Who" records that he was educated at "private schools, London; Switzerland; Mecklinburg-Schwerin; Birkbeck Institute; City of London College." Mr. Webb is said never to have illuminated his antecedents. It would appear to be unusual for an ordinary English hairdresser to educate his son in Switzerland and Germany.

A Fact-twisting Tract

In 1878 Sidney Webb became a clerk in the War Office, then a Surveyor of Taxes, and after that a clerk in the Colonial Office until he left the Civil

16

Service in 1891. During this time he wrote "Facts for Socialists" (Fabian Tract, No. 5), the most popular of the Fabian Society Tracts. The curious can find this tract dissected in Professor Hearnshaw's "Survey of Socialism."

"Of all the perpetual memorials of Fabian duplicity," says Professor Hearnshaw, "the notorious Tract No. 5 stands pre-eminent. It is an almost perfect model of the way in which authentic figures, drawn from reputable and authoritative sources, can be manipulated . . . to convey to ignorant and uncritical minds pernicious and inflammatory falsehoods."

In 1892 Mr. Webb married Miss Beatrice Potter, a lady who had been a pupil of Herbert Spencer. and who had just written a book on the co-operative movement. Her father was a wealthy railway magnate who died on January 1. 1892, leaving her a large fortune. This marriage, curiously, was one of the many pies in which Lord Haldane, then Mr. R. B. Haldane, had a finger. Lord Haldane relates in his autobiograhy that the two had become attracted to each other. but it was plain that Miss Potter's father would object to the engagement.

How Fabians Woo

"By their desire," says Lord Haldane, "I went more than once to stay at her father's house. He was then an invalid, bed-ridden and dying. I went, and, by arrangement, asked that my friend, Mr. Sidney Webb. who happened to be lecturing near there on the Saturday night at Stroud, might also come for the week end. The governess who was in charge thought that this was all right, because she put me down as the fortunate young man. She was old, and when she found us in the schoolroom late at night, she thought it was all as it should be, and retired leaving us to put out the lights. I then said, 'I must have a walk on the common alone, otherwise I shall not be able to sleep, and I can't be away for less than an hour.' This I did, and came back and found the happy couple had had a conversation which they could not otherwise have had Soon after that Mr. Potter, her father died. . .. I never belonged to the Fabian Society but was always very much in contact with Sidney Webb, and brought some of his ideas into the consultations which Asquith and Grey and I used to have on the future of Liberalism."

Lord Haldane's association with the intrigues preceding the Great War in 1914 is described in "All These Things" (A. N. Field, Nelson, N.Z., 6s.).

The Firm at Work

With his domestic affairs thus happily provided for, Mr. Webb gained an untiring helpmeet. He and Mrs. Webb jointly wrote a history of trades unionism; and they have sat on innumerable Royal Commissions, in drafting the reports of which they have played an important part. Mr. Webb on the London County Council, was most active in promoting municipal socialism. The economic system imposed on Russia by the Bolsheviks is very much as advocated by Mr. Webb in 1888. In 1919 Mr. Webb on the Royal Commission on the Coal Mines put in a complete scheme of nationalisation. He was President of the Board of Trade in the first Labour Government, and in 1929 he went to the House of Lords as Lord Passfield, being at the same time Secretary for the Dominions; his wife, however, insisting on remaining plain Mrs. Webb. As to whether Lord Passfield or Mrs. Webb is senior partner in the Firm of Webb, there is difference of opinion. Mr. Pease, secretary of the Fabian Society, said in his history that since 1912 Mrs. Webb had dominated .it.

V.

Artful Dodgers Sell Socialism

Mr. H. G. Wells, the Socialist novelist, once tried to wrest the leadership of the Fabian Society from the Webbs, who soon regained it. Mr. Wells later referred to Mr. Webb as an "incessant little intriguer". Mr. Wells said in the "Sunday Express" of December 11, 1927, that the Baileys in his novel "The New Machiavelli" were not the Webbs. "but only Webby people". In the novel one finds it written:

"I can still recall little Bailey, glib and winking, explaining that Democracy was really just a dodge for getting assent to the ordinances of the expert official by means of the polling booth."

Mr. H. G. Wells is also on record as saying of Fabian tactics of "permeation" that its leaders are "a very small group of pedants who believe that fair ends may be reached by foul means".

Engels himself, the partner of Marx, said of the Fabians in 1893: "Their tactics are to fight the Liberals not as decided opponents, but to drive them on to Socialistic consequences; therefore to trick them, to permeate Liberalism with Socialism, and not to oppose Socialistic candidates to Liberal ones, but to palm them off, to thrust them on, under some pretext. . . All is rotten."

"The Fabian Society," wrote Mr. Ellis Barker, "is the least open and least straightforward Socialist organisation. . . it habitually sails under a false flag, wishing not to arouse suspicion as to its objects. . . Fabians rely chiefly for their success upon their artfulness."

"This process of secret and gradual insinuation," said Dr. Beattie Crozier. "was, in effect, a real conspiracy"; and he called Mr. Webb the arch-conspirator and "sole High Pontiff of Fabian Socialism."

"Lord, What Fools These Liberals Be!"

As to how Fabians actually set about propagating Socialism. the following example of Fabian work, written by Mr. Bernard Shaw and recounting an exploit of his own, is taken from the "History of the Fabian Society." Armed with a programme drawn up by Sidney Webb. and which it was desired to palm off on to the Liberal Party, Mr. Shaw set out. He relates:

"I being then a permeative Fabian on the St. Pancras Liberal and Radical Association (I had coolly walked in and demanded to be elected to the Association and Executive, which was done on the spot by the astonished Association—ten strong or thereabouts), took them down to a meeting in Percy Hall, Percy Street, Tottenham Court Road, where the late Mr. Beale, then Liberal candidate and subscription milch cow of the constituency (without a ghost of a chance) was to address as many of the ten as might turn up under the impression he was addressing a public meeting.

"There were certainly not twenty present, perhaps not ten. I asked him to move the resolutions. He said they looked complicated, and that if I would move them he would second them. I moved them, turning over Webb's pages by batches, and not reading most of them. Mr. Beale seconded. Passed unanimously.

"That night they went down to the 'Star' with a report of an admirable speech which Mr. Beale was supposed to have delivered. Next day he found the National Liberal Club in an uproar at the revolutionary break-away. But he played up . . . said we lived in progressive times and must move with them."

This incident is typical of the tricks and dodges by which British Liberalism was pushed along towards Socialistic policies.

Tricky Propaganda

Professor Hearnshaw points out that the essential dishonesty of the Fabians is their persistent and continuous representation of Collectivism as Socialism. They always represent such things as the Post Office and the State schools as examples of Socialism, and suggest that, having started, the nation may as well go the whole hog. At the same time they keep out of sight the real central fact that their Socialistic objective is the EXTINCTION of private enterprise. They keep on at this class of propaganda in spite of endless exposures.

"These men," says Professor Hearnshaw, "are not ignoramuses; they include some of the masters of the art and craft of letters, experts in the exact use of language. It is difficult, indeed, to acquit them of the charge of deliberate deception."

In 1935 Mr. and Mrs. Webb published a book of 1143 pages in defence of Bolshevism. It was entitled "Soviet Communism: A New Civilisation". A section is devoted to "explaining" away the ruthlessness of Bolshevism, and the job is done in a truly slithery Fabian way. Here is a sample:

"No one can compute the sum of human suffering caused by this triple revolution over so vast an area, in so brief a time, amid the most embittered civil war, supported by half a dozen foreign armies actually invading Soviet territory.

"But equally no one can compute the sum of human suffering even unto the death, caused in England by the Protestant Reformation, the Industrial Revolution, and the triumph of democratic parliamentarianism, the whole drawn out over four centuries, with only the mildest of civil wars, and with next to no foreign wars."

This is the sort of dope by which Socialism has been propagated and by which Bolshevism is being whitewashed. Fabianism has taken the naked ugliness of the Marxian gospel of loot and slaughter and wrapped it up in a napkin to trade it off on the British people. The massacres of the Russian people by the Bolsheviks were part and parcel of their programme of terror. Their rule has throughout rested upon terrorism. But the Fabian adroitly waves away everything inconvenient.

Accoucheurs to Labour Party

In Bernard Shaw's account of his palming off of a Fabian policy on the St. Pancras Liberals printed above, the Fabian contempt for the people they were making use of appears very clearly. One looks in vain for a similar free and frank account in the Fabian official history of how Socialism was sold to Britain's trade unions by the Fabian Society. The Fabians were through with the Liberals when the book was written, but it was still advisable not to laugh too loudly over exploits in trades union quarters.

The story of the capture of the British Labour movement for Socialism has to be sought in other quarters. Of the part of "the Firm of Webb" therein, we have the statement of the Jew Laski of their London School of Economics: "Nor will anyone know until its archives are examined by a competent historian, how immense were their services in bringing the Labour Party to birth."

VI

Cuckoos in the Labour Nest

The Marx-Engels clique, founders of Bolshevism (though they never lived to see their doctrine under that name) were direct creators of Labour Socialism in Britain. Down to the early nineties trade unions were run on democratic principles, and were devoted to securing better working conditions for their members.

Socialism was unknown in trade unionism in those days. William Morris in 1883 commented on the fact that a Socialist could not get a hearing from a labour audience. As late as 1890 the Socialistic Professor W. Graham was saying, "The English working classes are not Socialists, nor are they very promising materials out of which to make Socialists."

Things were stirring at this date, however, and Engels was stirring them. In the New York Public Library is a mass of letters between Marx Engels, and a German Communist, F. A. Sorge. Sorge published some of these in 1906, but photostats of the originals made for Lieut.-Col. A. H. Lane, author of "The Alien Menace", show that Sorge omitted much that was illuminating. An expert who examined the documents in full reported to Colonel Lane:

"What is particularly noticeable in the letters of Engels and Marx is the contempt of those Communists for the mentality and characters of British 'labour' leaders, and most of our so-called statesmen. Their plan for causing a bloody revolution in our islands appears to have been based on a belief that the British working men and working women were fools."

How They Loved Each Other

However, this bunch of revolutionaries were not polite even about one another, as may be seen from E. H. Carr's "Karl Marx". Lassalle, for instance—the hanger-on of a rich countess nineteen years older than himself—sends Marx money. Is Marx grateful? Not a bit! Marx takes the cash and carries on in letters to Engels, referring to Lassalle as "weasel-beast", the "Jewish nigger", and so on. Lassalle on holiday picks up with another woman, and is killed in a duel in consequence. Marx thereupon writes to the rich countess (with an obvious

23

eye on the cash-box), saying he is "shocked and shattered"; Lassalle was one for whom he had "a great affection": "no one can feel deeper grief than I . . . I loved him personally," etc., etc. Then Marx sits down and writes to Engels: "The air needs purifying . . . from this stale stink of Lassalle." Such was the path-finder to the paradise of Socialism!

Three years after Marx's death things were moving with the Engels-Marx clique, consisting then of Engels, Eleanor Marx, Marx's youngest daughter, known as "Tussy", and her "husband", Professor Aveling (whom she never legally married). In her "Socialist Network", Mrs. Webster prints a translation of a letter from Engels to Sorge, under date of May 4, 1887:

"Aveling is making a famous agitation in the East End of London . . . he and Tussy are hard at work. It is a matter of founding an English Labour Party with an independent class programme."

Engels Finds a Tool

Soon Engels was writing that the Gas Workers and General Labourers were being "bossed by Tussy". In 1892 Engels reported great progress in England. Says Mrs. Webster: "In January of the following year, 1893, the Independent Labour Party was founded under the leadership of Engels' tool, Keir Hardie, whom he contemptuously described as an 'over-sly Scot' . . . and 'a poor devil of a Scotch miner'." Engels, thus poking his hand into British Labour matters, be it noted, had never even been naturalised, and lived in England under the protection of the German Government, of which there is strong suspicion he was a secret agent.

From 1890, in which year it had been busy "permeating" the trades unions in Lancashire, the Fabian Society had been paying much attention to the Labour movement. It joined with the Social Democratic Federation to help float off the Independent

Labour Party, and local Fabian Societies which had been formed among trade unionists turned themselves into I.L.P. branches. Unlike the Fabian Society, the I.L.P. was openly Socialist. Its methods generally, however, were underhand, as witness the following description by an old railway trades unionist who vigorously resisted the Socialist onslaught. The extract is from Mr. W. V. Osborne's "Sane Trades Unionism":

Boring from Within

"The Independent Labour Party, more commonly known as the I.L.P. was formed in 1893 for the express purpose of permeating other organisations with Socialist doctrine. Recognising their own inability to organise, they sought to use the already existing societies, and on account of this earned the name of the political cuckoos.

"Their first step was to form a Socialist group within the various Unions and branches of Unions. They kept in touch with the central body, and meeting in secret conclave arranged their course of action. They attended regularly, and took a prominent part in the work of the branch, while the ordinary member was often apathetic and irregular in attendance. Resolutions were prepared previous to the meetings, and the supporters were always ready to play their part, so that the organised minority easily- out-manoeuvred the unorganised majority.

"Branch officers who had served their societies well and faithfully for years became victims to this campaign. The edict had gone forth to capture the official positions, and this was done in the most unscrupulous manner.

"At a private meeting of the Socialist section, nominations would be decided upon for the different positions, nominators and seconders would be arranged, and often a fierce attack would be made upon the holder of the coveted position. Canvassing would go on outside the branch, quietly, and in such an indirect manner as not to expose the real purpose. The candidate would drop all talk of Socialism, and in some cases even repudiate it. The person to be driven from office, being wholly unconscious of the coming attack, would make no effort to organise support.

Back-stairs Schemers

"For a seat on the Executive Committee, or for a delegation to an annual congress, where it was necessary for the candidate to obtain support from a number of branches, the Socialist groups in the different districts were kept in touch with each other through the central Socialist organisation. Their victory was rendered easier by limiting the number of candidates for any particular office, while the other members put forward numerous candidates, split their votes, and lost. Even after the election the plot was rarely discovered, all that was apparent being that an old officer had been replaced by a more active member.

"Once in possession of the official positions the same means was used for the manipulation of the machinery. Important matters were placed either at the top or the bottom of the agenda, so that they could be rushed through before many members had arrived or after the majority of the ordinary members had left.

"By such means the Unions were gradually drawn from the pursuit of purely industrial to political objects. No opportunity was lost to advance the Socialist propaganda. The Trade Unionist was taught that the true function of the Unions was not collective bargaining as between employer and employed, but rather the waging of a class war in by which the employer—the supposed enemy of the worker—was to be suppressed. . .

"The fundamental principle of present day Trade

Unionism appears to be class war, a war that appeals to the worst passions of human nature. It is not surprising that a movement built upon such a foundation should produce a deteriorating effect on individual character."

Prominent in the I.L.P., under the leadership of Keir Hardie, were Tom Mann, J. Ramsay Mac-Donald, Philip Snowden, J. R. Clynes, G. N. Barnes, Bruce Glasier, G. H. Roberts, and, Robert Blatchford.

VII

The Conquest of the Unions

As early as 1893 in a "Joint Manifesto of British Socialist Bodies"—comprising the I.L.P., Fabian Society, and the Social Democratic Federation—Communism was adopted as the objective.

"Our aim, one and all," said the Manifesto, "is to obtain for the whole community complete ownership and control of the means of transport, the means of manufacture, the mines and the land. Thus we look to put an end for ever to the wage system, to sweep away all distinctions of class, and eventually to establish national and international Communism on a sound basis."

The only thing left out of the full Marxian programme was the use of violence to effect the proclaimed ends. Had this been included, however, it would have been useless even to have attempted to sell Socialism to Britons. But the Socialists have never ceased to show their sympathy with those who do use force for the attainment of these ends. "That which is generally called Socialism," said Lenin in "The State and Revolution", "is termed by Marx the first or lower phrase of Communist society."

By 1899 Socialist penetration of the Trades Unions was so far advanced that at the Trades

Union Congress of that year a resolution was successfully put through inviting the co-operation of "all Co-operative Societies, Socialistic, and other working-class organisations" in devising means for increased Labour representation in Parliament. This resulted in a conference in 1900 attended by delegates representing respectively 545,316 trades unionists and 22,861 Socialists. This conference set up a Labour Representation Committee with a standing executive.

A Tricky Constitution

The first move of the Socialists was to prevent this Labour Representation Committee from becoming a committee of the Trade Union Congress. If this had happened membership would have been restricted to trades unionists and paid officials of trade unions. The Socialists manoeuvred things so that this supposedly democratic movement had an executive committee of which seven members represented 545,316 trade unionists, while 22,861 Socialists got five members. Further, Socialists who were trade unionists could vote in their trade unions and also in their Socialist societies, thus gaining double representation. The path to minority control was thus neatly prepared.

In 1903 Mr. Keir Hardie, leader of the I.L.P., showed how democratic Socialism was by saying on March 3: "If the old gang of trade unionists should get in on a majority on the Labour Representation Committee Party, the Independent Labour Party, which existed for the making of Socialists, would revert to its original position." Socialist contempt for those whom they use is here again seen.

Mr. James Ramsay MacDonald became the first secretary of the Labour Representation Committee. He was never a trade unionist, but came along to the conference with the Fabian and I.L.P. bunch of Socialists.

Two James MacDonalds

It has been asserted that Mr. Ramsay MacDonald's election was a carefully engineered affair, framed up by the Fabian Society and the I.L.P. At any rate Mr. H. M. Hyndman, leader of the Social Democratic Federation, wrote as follows in his "Further Reminiscences" (Macmillan, 1912):

"As to Mr Ramsay MacDonald, he is not a man I care to waste much space on. I have seen a good deal of him at various times. . . Personal ambition has been his one motive throughout. . . A man who had never done a day's work as a manual labourer in his life, who was not and did not pretend to be a trade unionist, who was then working as a Liberal journalist, who had been a Scotch schoolmaster, and was at the time, I believe, also private secretary to that very earnest Radical M.P., Mr. Thomas Lough, was elected unanimously as first unpaid secretary to the newly formed political Labour Party. It seemed quite incredible that this should have occurred. . .

"I was told that most of those who voted for this smart middleclass manipulator as secretary thought they were voting for the James MacDonald who moved the Socialist resolution, and that, the two Social-Democratic delegates being absent during this important vote, there was no one present to put the matter right. That the stroke must have been carefully engineered beforehand is quite certain, and what has gone on ever since gives rather a sinister complexion to the whole manoeuvre."

Conservatism Bird-limed, Too

Ramsay MacDonald, who thus played a prominent part in the manipulations by which the British Labour movement was successfully trapped into Socialism, was the leading figure on the stage thirty-one years later in the intrigue that entangled the British Conservative Party in the same noxious

29

toils. As might be expected, it was pressure by the secret owners of the Bank of England that led to the crazy alliance in 1931 of the British Conservatives with the MacDonald Socialists, which alliance represents the crowning achievement of Jewish Marxist penetration in Britain to date.

It is curious to note that the impression Ramsay MacDonald made at the outset of his political career on his fellow-Socialist H. M. Hyndman, was almost exactly that which he left with his colleague Philip Snowden after the events of 1931. In his autobiography (1934), Lord Snowden referred to Mr. MacDonald's "passion for intrigue and compromise, and his desire to be regarded as a 'gentleman' by the other parties."

Lord Snowden related that Mr. MacDonald "set about the formation of a National Government with an enthusiasm which showed that the adventure was wholly to his mind," adding that: "He had always entertained a feeling of something like contempt for the Trade Union leaders."

Unions Milked for Money

Throughout the whole history of Socialism the student finds a widespread feeling that its propagators are all the time playing up to the masses for ulterior ends. The story is one of continual and endless intrigue and deception under cover of highfaluting talk about "Democracy", "Humanitarianism", and similar phrases.

In 1906 the Labour Representation Committee changed its name to the Labour Party, but its constitution remained the same, except that the Social Democratic Federation dropped out at an early date. The executive committee remained at twelve members, with nine appointed by the trade unions and three by the tiny Socialist bodies (two by the I.L.P. and one by the Fabian Society). "The Trades Unionists on the Committee," writes Mr. Pease in his "History of the Fabian Society", "represented in the earlier years about 100,000 members each. I then represented some 700 (Fabians)."

"The Socialist movement in this country," wrote Mr. Richard Bell, Labour M.P. and secretary of the great Amalgamated Society of Railway Servants, in his little book on "Trade Unionism" in 1907, "has not grown up much on its own merits. While it was confined to Socialist organisations, its progress was very slow. . . The formation of the Labour Party, and of its compulsory maintenance fund, has been a good thing for these Socialist organisations. The bargain from their standpoint is no doubt a good one; they largely dominate the policy, whilst the Trade Unions provide the funds."

Riding on Labour's Back

Mr. Bell pointed out that the Socialists had been getting far more than their share of the nominations for Parliamentary candidatures. The trades unionists were not Socialists but by 1907 they had been astutely manoeuvred into putting up the money to pay the salaries of seven Socialist members of Parliament and to defray their election expenses. Trade unionists who did not support these Socialists were branded as "traitors". The Socialist tail had begun well and truly to wag the trade union dog.

"The Socialists had moved very discreetly," wrote Mr. W. V. Osborne, another trade unionist in his "Sane Trade Unionism", "always covering their movements by plausible language, and progressing step by step towards a definite goal—the complete control of the Trade Union machinery for the advancement of Socialist candidatures. . . No man, not a Socialist, was allowed to act for himself in political matters, but was compelled to accept the instructions issued from headquarters . . . Since the Socialists had captured most of the official union positions, they controlled all means of communication not only as between union and union, but also as between branch and branch."

VIII

The Ideal and the Real

By 1908 Socialist penetration of the trade unions was sufficiently advanced to secure a vote committing the Labour Party to Socialism. At the outset the Labour Party was ostensibly set up because it was necessary for the trade unions "to use their political power to defend their existence": and anything in the way of party politics was deprecated. At the 1908 conference a Social Democratic delegate moved that the objects of the Labour Party should be:

"The overthrow of the present competitive system of capitalism and the institution of a system of public ownership and control of all the means of life."

This proposal was defeated by 951,000 votes to 91,000. Nevertheless, two days later the same conference passed a resolution differently worded but just as Socialistic, adopting as its main objective:

"The socialisation of the means of production, distribution, and exchange, to be controlled by a democratic State in the interest of the entire community."

This is the Marxian programme. It means the extinction of all private enterprise, and is necessarily destructive of all freedom. Everyone under such a system will be an employee of the State. Every man's career will depend on the opinion of him formed by his superiors. Those superiors, it is true, are to be elected by the people to act in the interests of the people.

Slave-State Trap

Superficially, this SOUNDS well. Actually, what does it mean. It means that any man who opposes the rulers of a fully Socialist State opposes

32

his employers. on whose goodwill towards him his advancement in life depends. If he offends those employers he is devoid of the means of living, for everything is in the control of these officials.

What will be the position of a man employed by the State and elected to Parliament under such circumstances? Even if his position as a member is financially secure during his period in the legislature, any criticism he makes is a criticism of those who have been, and may again be, his official superiors.

If such a member discovers and discloses corruption or favouritism in the administration, or advocates policies disliked by the administration, where will he stand? The newspapers and printing presses in a Socialistic State will be entirely in the hands of the ruling officials whom he is opposing and exposing. With all the machinery of publicity in the hands of the ruling officials, would a critical and rebellious M.P. get much of a hearing? He would be a lucky man not to be blacklisted for life.

In Russia after twenty years of Marxist rule the first elections were held in December 1937, and in the whole 160 millions of people under Bolshevik rule only two men came forward and contested seats against the official candidates. In 1141 constituencies there was no candidate but the nominee of the ruling officials.

Socialism's Heaven on Earth

A former Soviet Commissar, and now repentant Communist, Morris Gordin, Chief of the Press Bureau of the Moscow International up to 1924, in his address in Detroit in 1931 already quoted, thus described how Marxism works out in practice:

"The Communist Party is a supreme trust owning everything in Russia . . . It is the fist which represents the Soviet's ideology, brute power . . . I looked into the matter and I saw definitely that the voting of the resolutions and everything was not

33

done by the rank and file of the party. It was the Tcheka which told the party what to do . . . To-day they suppress all free thought. They suppress not only thought, in fact they have decapitated the nation. They took the head off the Russian people; they butchered every independent intellectual; they exiled hundreds of professors, and any man who tries to think for himself in any degree is an infidel; he is a counter-revolutionist, if he does not agree with any Commissar in the Tcheka. In thinking, in writing, the military censorship tells you how to write, how to think. But, even more than that, what to write upon what subjects. This means there is no science in Russia but the science of Revolution; there is no religion but the religion of Satan, of Leninism, and this forms the basis of Proletarian Kultur . . . To-day nobody is participating in the Soviet Government except the officials of it, the select henchmen of one man, Stalin, the super-tyrant and bureaucrat, the Emperor of the Soviet Dictatorship, the Tsar of the Proletarian Red Empire."

Socialists Plot Dictatorship

In Britain the Socialists, having attained their present position by the methods we have noted, exhibited the humbug of their talk of Democracy very clearly in 1933 and 1934. In the former year the then newly-formed Socialist League section of the Labour Party passed resolutions urging that a Labour Government on coming into office should at once introduce an Emergency Powers Act, setting up a dictatorship. Sir Stafford Cripps and Professor Laski were leading advocates of this.

At the Labour Party annual conference in 1934 the leaders of the Labour Party and the Socialist League met in private, and Sir Stafford Cripps later stated in the open conference that agreement had been reached in the matter, and the emergency powers dictatorship proposal had been adopted.

Democracy the Burglar's Ladder

Democracy, for Socialists, is merely a ladder by which to get control of the State: Dictatorship is what you do after you get there. The entire Socialist programme is nothing but humbug, trickery and deceit, from top to bottom. It is the concoction of aliens kicked out of their own countries, and its propagation throughout has been by methods of underhand cunning. It is essentially irreligious, and through the Great War its leading advocates played a traitor's part.

A Nice Proposition!

Behind this movement all the time there is Money. Money was poured out like water to put over the Bolshevik revolution in Russia. This trail of Money is found running everywhere. Take the case of Mr. George Lansbury, late chairman of the British Labour Party. In his book "Looking Backwards and Forwards" (Blackie, 1935) this pillar of British Socialism relates how Sir Samuel Montagu, later Lord Swaythling, of the great international family of moneylending Jews (original name Samuel), gave him money to keep strikes going. Mr. Lansbury adds:

"In this and other ways Montagu and I seemed likely to be in a long partnership. We parted politically, however, when I became a definite Socialist . . . When Sir Samuel heard of this he asked me to see him at the House of Commons . . . Sir Samuel was kindness itself, and reminded me of what he had said at King's College, which was that he would get me a seat in the House of Commons at the earliest opportunity. Meantime, why not (he said) think of my wife and family, and the good I could do by remaining with the Liberal Party and preaching my Socialism inside it! He ended by offering me the position of agent for him in Whitechapel at quite a good salary. But this was not to be, and we parted . . . All the same, we at home never for a moment entertained anything but the highest respect for this extremely wealthy man."

Another Queer Transaction

The reader must ask himself why this wealthy Jewish financier wished to have Socialism preached inside the Liberal Party of which he was a member. And he may further ask for what reason the wealthy Jewish soapmaker of Philadelphia, Joseph Fels put up money in 1907 to finance Lenin and Trotsky. Mr. Lansbury in that year secured for the Russian Revolutionary party the use of the Brotherhood Church in Hackney for their conference, and in his book he says: "It was Joseph Fels who out of sheer love of humanity put down the money they needed. This money was repaid by Lenin immediately the Bolsheviks seized power."

Trotsky in his "History of the Russian Revolution" in referring to this episode says: "An English Liberal agreed to lend the Russian Revolution three thousand pounds as nearly as I can remember the figure." The London "Patriot" of November 2, 1933, says that according to Mrs. Fels the sum was £1800, and according to Israel Zangwill it was £17,000. "This little man," says Mr. Lansbury, "travelled Great Britain, Ireland and Denmark, interviewing kings and princes, premiers, cabinet ministers, and the clergy, pouring out his money like water." Incidentally, Mr. Fels lavishily entertained Keir Hardie, Mr. Lansbury and other Socialist leaders.

Britons, if they have regard for their own welfare, will be extremely well advised to support political doctrines more distinctly concerned with the promotion of British interests, and more British in principles and methods, than ever Socialism has been, or is likely to be.

Printed by Alfred George Betts, of Kawai Street, Nelson at his registered printing office, Hardy Street, Nelson, New Zealand.

EXAMINER

An Independent National Bulletin.

Edited by A. N. Field.

The Examiner contains a monthly budget of news throwing light on the operation of the forces making for war and revolution throughout the world.

The matter is carefully collated from a wide variety of sources, and provides a mass of information not appearing in the daily newspapers.

Each month a supplement deals at length with some special topic. This pamphlet is a reprint of one such supplement: others will shortly be re-issued in pamphlet form.

Subscription: Three Shillings a Year posted anywhere.

A. N. Field, Box 154, Nelson, New Zealand.

Stabilised Money

1s 6d. posted.

A readable statement of the case for money reform made by A. N. Field before the N.Z. Government Monetary Committee in 1934, with cross-examination thereon.

"Of great value to all interested in currency and credit questions: it contains much that is unknown to the general public both here and in America."—London "Patriot", August 23, 1934.

"I find 'Stabilised Money' very amusing and interesting, as well as instructive. The form of discussion, question and answer, brings out the points clearly, sometimes with grim humour."—An Englishwoman active in public affairs.

A. N. Field, Box 154, Nelson, New Zealand.